pests

Charlie Ryrie

Gaia Books Ltd

CONTENTS

PREFACE

Soil Association

The membership charity
campaigning for an organic Britain

The use of chemical insecticides to rid a garden of insect pests is not an option for the organic grower and gardener. Not only do such products destroy the intended target but they also damage the fragile ecological balance that is necessary to maintain a healthy, productive garden. Observe if you will, the list of precautions printed on every packet of pesticide or fungicide and consider their implications. Many products of this type, judged safe in years gone by, have now been proved to be too dangerous for us to use and so we must learn to deal with pests in a completely different way. There are strategies available to gardeners that avoid any need to board the pesticide treadmill and most require a deeper knowledge of the habits and life-cycles of the garden foes we all encounter. Know your enemy!

Without the chemical option, organic gardening relies on close observation and knowledge. It may seem a daunting task to control pests but taking the time to examine plants for pests and to look for beneficial pests brings the gardener into a much closer and more rewarding relationship with his plot. No longer is it an object to be controlled into a state of perfection, but a realm of myriad creatures and plants, all playing their part in a complex world that can be in perfect balance. For it is true that the longer one practices organic gardening methods, the less one needs to do anything at all about pests. Their numbers dwindle to a level that does not need to be dealt with, kept from population explosions by the other creatures in the web of wildlife in the garden.

This book introduces many tried and tested organic methods of pest control, from ways to encourage garden friends and adjusting planting times to creating physical barriers between plants and pests.

Rob Hayward
Horticultural Development Officer
The Soil Association

Organic management and control of garden pests and diseases has become more and more popular in recent years. Old-fashioned chemicals, once seen as the lynchpin of garden management, have declined in popularity as gardeners have become aware of potential long-term damage to human health, and to the environment.

Over-reliance on pesticides has caused many insect species to develop resistance, which has resulted in the need for yet more powerful chemicals to be developed. This in turn has led in some cases to decimation of the population of natural predators. Many gardens have consequently suffered pest and disease problems as a result of using available chemicals.

Organic pest and disease management encourages a balance in the garden. A certain level of pest attack is tolerated as this allows nature's efficient system of checks and balances to operate. Natural predators exist in a wide range of environments. The gardener can rely on allies ranging from beneficial soil-dwelling bacteria to aphid-devouring insects. When used in conjunction with traps, barriers, and a small number of botanically based sprays, the organic gardener has all the means needed to maintain the health and vigour of every type of plant.

HDRA, the organic organisation, is one of the oldest environmental organisations. It researches, promotes and advises on organic cultivation for home gardeners everywhere. It works to continually improve composting, pest and disease control and other techniques, to enable organic gardeners to produce better crops of sturdy, healthy vegetables, fruits and ornamentals.

the organic organisation

An international membership organisation, researching and promoting organic horticulture and agriculture

Maggi Brown
Senior Adviser
HDRA, the organic organisation

WHY

USE ORGANIC METHODS?

Chemical pesticides don't work. They offer an instant fix that simply makes the problem of pests worse in the long run. Pesticides destroy nature's system of checks and balances, while an organic approach means that you can use the plants and creatures in your garden to help keep unwanted visitors under control.

CONTROLLING YOUR GARDEN

'If it moves, kill it' has been too popular for too long. Gardeners who follow this school of thought may end up with a shiny tidy garden, but the only way they'll keep that up is through ever-increasing arrays of toxic chemicals. Once you start using artificial ways of maintaining your garden, it's far too easy to become reliant on them, and create a vicious circle. Using chemical pesticides may seem a simple way of killing or controlling pests, but pesticides do not solve the complex problem of maintaining a healthy balance in your garden. Chemicals don't only remove pests, they destroy creatures that you do want in your garden. They are like any drug: they artificially prop up a system for a short while, but in the longer term they will destroy your garden's health.

Checks and balances

Don't rush to exterminate too much life in your garden. There's a reason why it's there. Biological controls have always existed to keep pests down, as pests are also food sources for creatures that may pollinate your flowers, or eat debris, or keep other pests off your plants, or keep the soil in good condition, or a thousand and one other helpful functions. A healthy garden will contain plenty of pest predators: some beneficial creatures eat the pests, others lay their eggs inside host insect pests; bacteria in the soil can poison some pests. If you kill off the population of one 'pest' species there will be no food for the predators that need it, and they will also die, so their beneficial functions won't be performed and so on. The knock-on effects of chemical pesticide use in a garden can be frighteningly far-reaching.

Soil life

Your soil contains thousands of organisms working together to keep it healthy and fertile. Worms and insects drag rotting material down into the soil, digest and excrete it and transform it into plant food, with the help of soil bacteria, fungi and algae. When synthetic pesticides get into your soil they kill off these important organisms that are responsible for keeping your soil healthy and releasing plant nutrients. This means that nutrients in the soil are not made available and plants can't get at them, so your plants become weaker until they can't support themselves. Gardeners then become ever more reliant on artificial inputs – chemical fertilisers, herbicides and more pesticides – just to keep things going. But there's no need.

Pesticides create pest problems

Pesticides can make a pest situation worse. If you keep applying pesticides, the intended pests will eventually adapt or become resistant to the chemicals you are throwing at them. Or secondary pests that are not affected by the chemicals will become primary pests. So more and different chemicals have to be developed to get rid of the secondary pest, adding to the existing cocktail of chemicals that is being released into your garden, harming plants and soil as well as pests. Blanket application of pesticides doesn't stop at killing pests, it also kills life that you need in your garden.

The need for control

A garden is not a natural environment, and some pests can cause problems, but there are safe and effective ways to keep them from damaging your garden. It is always best to strike before any problem appears, and many natural ways of pest control are common sense practices, such as giving your plants the conditions they prefer. Some helpful planting schemes rely on centuries of gardeners' observations. Biological methods of control mimic processes at work in nature, and botanical pesticides break down without harming the environment. Or you can get physical and use traps and barriers.

Agricultural (and horticultural) pesticides are made from petrochemicals, based on oil, a non-renewable resource. Modern agricultural processes are very oil-energy intensive, in the fuel they use directly to power machinery and fuel used indirectly to make fertilisers and pesticides. This is estimated at 2.6% of total energy usage in the UK.

Pesticides don't just harm the environment by indiscriminate killing of pests and predators, plants and organisms. By polluting watercourses and sources and poisoning animals, they accumulate in the environment. The organophosphate and organochlorine families of pesticides don't break down easily, so although organisms at the bottom of the food chain absorb tiny quantities of the chemicals, these increase as you go higher up the food chain.

WHAT

SHOULD I DO TO CONTROL PESTS?

Throw away sprays and start to think organic. Learn how good garden practices and specific planting can encourage natural biological controls. Find ways of excluding pests, so they never become a problem, and safely destroying those that do cause damage.

WHAT MEASURES CAN I TAKE?

Organic pest control isn't about swapping chemical sprays for organic ones. It is an integrated approach where you help your garden to help you. Organic gardening means an increased awareness of the processes at work in your garden, and recognising how best to work with them. This awareness helps you to notice pests before they escalate to problem levels. Organic sprays are available, but they should be used only as a last resort. The most effective agent of pest control in any organic garden is always you, the gardener.

There is no substitute for building and maintaining a healthy soil, for considered planting and constant vigilance. The most important organic pest control is simply good gardening practice.

Organic gardening means creating a garden that can help support itself, so the most important way of controlling pests is by good gardening practice.

General measures
A well-structured soil that is full of organic matter will support strong plants, and pests first attack weaker specimens. Fertile soil will also provide plenty of food for many flying, crawling and burrowing creatures so they will be less instantly attracted to your cultivated plants. If your soil is well-enriched with garden compost this provides an additional measure of protection as nutrient enriched soil surpresses soil borne pests and diseases.

Cultivation
Match your choice of plants to your garden. If, for example, you try and grow Mediterranean plants in a cold wet soil you'll never have much success and the plants will be weak and susceptible to every pest and disease that's doing the rounds. Test your pH regularly to make sure the soil is around neutral, and add lime if it is too acid for your chosen plants, or more compost if it has too much lime.

Plants stressed by excessive wind or weather will be weak and vulnerable so make sure they are adequately protected. Use companion planting (see page 26) for support and shade, and to encourage beneficial insects.

Diversity
Grow a diversity of plants in the conditions they like in order to keep your soil healthy and to support a wide range of garden life. If you concentrate on one or two species you are asking for problems as pests will have no difficulty getting stuck in. But if you grow a good mixture of plants they will attract a wide range of insects and other organisms so the predators/pests ratio should be

reasonably balanced and nature's system of checks and balances will be able to operate.

Encourage pest predators
Learn which creatures destroy pests (see pages 18-25) and encourage them into the garden by providing the plants and conditions they prefer. Provide them with friendly habitats, including sources of water and hiding places if necessary.

Physical measures
You may need to devise barriers and traps to keep pests out. These can be simple measures such as netting trees and soft fruit to prevent bird damage, covering crops with horticultural fleece to keep flying insects off or erecting fences or solid barriers to deter other pests. Basic sticky traps are useful against some pests, while biological warfare is relevant for others – pheromone traps lure insects with the scent of sex, but it's all simulated.

Introduce biological controls
If you can't get pest attack under control with cultivation, traps or barriers, other options are possible as a last resort. Microbial pesticides are made from bacteria that occur naturally in the soil. Or there are pesticides made from petals, seeds and roots, or sprays from soaps and natural oils.

Tolerance
Decide which pests you can tolerate, and those you can't. Something that seems reasonable to one gardener might drive another one crazy. I 've learnt to live with a level of slug destruction but flea beetles drive me to distraction. I can cope with birds but I can't bear badgers. Concentrate on what bothers you most.

Some insects breed incredibly fast – the common housefly can lay 600 eggs at a time which hatch out in 6 days. So over the course of one summer one pair of flies could produce enough offspring to cover the whole surface of the Earth several layers thick. But this doesn't happen. Biological controls exist. You can take advantage of the natural cycles of pests and predators for pest control in your garden.

CULTIVATING A PEST-FREE GARDEN

Good gardening practice
• Get the soil right
• Choose plants that fit your site
• Choose resistant varieties
• Plant a mixture of species
• Start plants in modules to give them a head start
• Intercrop
• Practise rotation
• Clear the ground in autumn rather than leaving pests to overwinter on stumps of brassicas or in overwintering roots
• Always remove pest-affected leaves and vegetables and compost them in a hot heap rather than leaving them on the ground or on the plant.

Make sure the plants you choose are right for the site and give them what they need. Plants that suit your garden will be stronger and better able to withstand anything that tries to attack them. Stressed plants are more susceptible to pest attack, and less well able to deal with it.

You should also try to choose plants for pest resistance. Many old or 'heirloom' varieties of flowers and vegetables are more resistant than modern hybrids. As food plants have been increasingly bred to satisfy perceived current tastes, some of the genetic characteristics that once stood them in good stead against pests have disappeared – strong oils, resins and hairiness, for example. The same thing has happened with ornamentals: as they have been increasingly developed for specific aesthetic notions, little or no emphasis may be attached on retaining a plant's resistance to pests or diseases.

Diversity
In a vegetable bed, mix up the species. Pests spread fast along the same species, but if you mix vegetables with flowers and unrelated species it seems to put predatory insects off. It also looks attractive. Some companion planting is helpful (see page 26) as well as simply mixing crops. Intercropping is also good practice, so that the ground is always covered. This keeps soil in good condition, provides ground cover for useful predators such as ground beetles and centipedes, and keeps out weeds that can host pests.

Rotation
Never grow the same vegetable in the same place two years running, but practise some kind of rotation, however small your plot. Pests tend to be plant-specific, and they will overwinter in the soil where a particular species grew, so if you plant the same species the next year it becomes an instant foodcrop for the pests. Tidy beds in autumn, removing decaying plants, for the same reason.

ENCOURAGING PREDATORS

All insect pests have natural enemies. The use of these organisms to manage pests is known as biological control. The importance of natural enemies should never be over-emphasised, and conservation of natural enemies is a vitally important pest control strategy in any garden.

• Varied planting encourages pollinators and predators. Plant annual flowers such as marigolds and poppies among your vegetables, and edge beds with herbs.

• Encourage birds by planting dense native shrubs, and feed birds through the winter. They will eat hundreds of pests and their eggs.

• A pond will bring in a range of aquatic life including predatory dragonflies, frogs and toads.

• A pile of logs offers protection or a place to hibernate for many garden helpers including beetles, toads, frogs, slow worms and hedgehogs.

Some predatory insects eat other insects, some use other insects as hosts, laying eggs in their bodies which hatch out, killing the host. Other creatures eat slugs and snails, or help keep soil healthy so that pests are less likely to get established. If you take a wide view, even so-called pests are beneficial in some way, as all creatures are part of complex webs of food chains that support life on earth. So when we talk about beneficial garden insects, we mean 'beneficial to the gardener'. They won't completely rid your garden of pests, but they should stop any pest from getting out of control – and many predatory insects are also useful pollinators.

The importance of predators

Predatory insects are the lions and tigers of the insect world. They are voracious feeders, catching their prey and either crunching and chewing up their victims, or sucking out all their juices. The biological cycles of pests and predators will fit, given the right conditions in your garden. So predators should appear at the time when your garden needs them most, populations of predator and prey rising and falling in natural cycles. You can help these natural controls along a bit by attracting specific predators. Synthetic pesticides, on the other hand, destroy natural cycles. They kill off whole populations of pests so predators have nothing to feed on and they die, or they kill important predators along with pests.

Habitats

Most beneficial insects will appear naturally in your garden if you provide a diversity of plants and habitats. Keep your beds clear of decay that can host pests and diseases, but a very neat and tidy garden is an unwelcoming place for friends so leave places for them to hibernate and hide. Get to know which creatures are most helpful, provide them with food, water, and a comfortable home.

LADYBIRDS, BEETLES & CENTIPEDES

If pests such as aphids are really abundant, ladybirds will tend to graze on them, skimming the top off the population but not adequately suppressing them. So a diversity of predators is important, each with different feeding habits.

Centipedes eat small slugs as well as numerous insects. They are easy to tell apart from unhelpful millipedes as they scuttle very quickly and only have one pair of legs per body segment, while millipedes have two. Orange-brown, and usually around 2.5cm long, centipedes hide in dark damp places and hunt at night.

Ground beetle ▶

Most people know that ladybirds are good to have in your garden, because they eat greenfly and other aphids. Everybody recognises the adult black spotted red variety, but there are dozens of others including orange and yellow varieties with black spots and black ones with red spots. The larvae are less well known, but these small greyish black grubs with indistinct orange blotches are the most voracious aphid eaters.

Adult ladybirds hibernate in houses and hedgerows throughout the winter and then emerge to lay eggs in spring. One ladybird larva feeds for several weeks, eating up to 500 aphids before pupating for 4-5 days prior to becoming an adult ladybird. As well as aphids, adult ladybirds eat mealybugs, scale insects, whiteflies, mites and other insects.

You sometimes come across a colony of ladybirds in the wild, either hibernating or sluggishly re-awaking in spring. Don't be tempted to bring them back to your garden. Ladybirds migrate from under one kilometre to up to one hundred to hibernate. If they are moved when they are still hibernating they will either wake up to follow the nursery rhyme and 'fly away home', or they will stay sluggish, never waking up properly to feed. It appears that the ladybirds need to fly to burn off fat they have stored for the winter before they are hungry enough to feed again.

Other beetles

Ground or carabid beetles are shiny purple-black backed beetles up to 2.5cm long. You can find them among ground-cover plants, or hiding under rotting vegetation, or in mulches. They are mostly nocturnal, preying on slugs and caterpillars as well as smaller insect pests.

Slim and speedy rove beetles look like brown and black earwigs without pincers. They are found in compost piles and under mulches. They eat slugs and insect eggs and grubs in the soil.

HOVERFLIES & LACEWINGS

A colony of aphids usually contains some aphid shells with holes pierced in one end. This is a sign that predatory larvae have been at work.

Favourite hoverfly flowers

Buckwheat *Fagopyron esculentum*
Candytuft *Iberis spp.*
Cornflower/knapweed *Centaurea spp.*
Dill *Anethum graveolens*
Morning glory *Convolvulus tricolor*
Mints *Mentha spp.*
Phacelia *Phacelia tanacetifolia*
Poached egg plant *Limnanthes douglasii*

Hoverfly ▶

Ephemeral looking lacewings are among the most important insect predators in any garden. The adults are beautiful green or yellowish-green insects about 1.5cm long with gauze-like wings and golden eyes. An adult lives for 20 to 40 days, feeding on pollen, and honeydew secreted by aphids. Every day each female lacewing lays 10 to 30 eggs on small stalks so that the later developers aren't eaten by the larvae that mature earlier. These pale brown larvae are incredibly active predators. They look like miniature flattened alligators and are known as 'aphid lions' because they eat so many aphids, along with spider mites, thrips, mealybugs, small caterpillars and insect eggs.

Hoverflies

Hoverflies are also attractive insect predators, resembling small slim wasps. They mimic the markings of bees and wasps to protect themselves from attack by birds, spiders and other predators. But they are easy to tell apart as hoverflies are much smaller, hover steadily rather than darting up and down, and only have one pair of wings.

Like lacewings, adult hoverflies are nectar and pollen feeders and it is their larvae that gobble up aphids. These are brown or green, without jointed legs, and can often be found among aphid colonies, puncturing aphids' skin and sucking out the liquid contents.

Flower feeders

Lacewings and hoverflies are busy feeders and pollinators and particularly at risk from pesticides used on flowering plants. So use the insects to control your aphids, and if things get out of hand try controlling an aphid population explosion with a soap and water spray (page 36) rather than resorting to measures such as botanicals (page 34).

You can buy lacewing hotels to attract them into your garden, but they will only stay and breed if you include a good variety of attractant plants.

BIRDS & MAMMALS, TOADS & FROGS

Don't destroy ants' nests as they are
a favourite late summer food of
green woodpeckers.

People used to think that toads could
give you warts, probably because of
the bumps on their skin that look like
warts. These bumps contain poison
that irritates the mouth of any
predators who try to eat toads. Be
careful in handling toads and always
wash your hands afterwards.

Toad ▶

Birds are both friends and pests, but they do more good than harm so you should try and welcome them. Their habit of stealing your fruit, seeds and young seedlings can drive you to distraction, but there are ways to foil them (see page 56), and they are also very helpful. Birds feed on hundreds of different pests at different stages of development – including really troublesome pests such as slugs and snails, codling moth, cutworms and wireworms, and they aerate the soil where they pierce it with their beaks to seek insects.

Bats
If you have bats in your garden, don't scare them away. They will eat thousands of insects in one night, and their droppings make very rich fertiliser. They are also the most effective controllers of summer biting insects such as mosquitoes and midges, as they come out to feed at about the time the biters get most active.

Hedgehogs
Hedgehogs are very greedy feeders – they eat slugs, milli-pedes and many pest grubs, but they are not particularly choosy, and will also eat beneficial insects and even small mammals and birds' eggs. Encourage them into your gar-den with suitable hibernation sites such as log piles, but don't treat them as pets and feed them or they won't do their job as pest controllers. Hedgehogs love beer so don't use beer traps (see page 33) when they're about.

Toads and frogs
Try to provide frogs and toads with a pond, and some dark damp places where they can hide and hibernate. Frogs feed predominantly off slugs, and toads also include numerous insects, woodlice and ants in their diet. Toads and frogs burrow under plant material in the winter, or under upturned flower pots.

SPIDERS, SLOW WORMS & WASPS

Spiders

Spiders have many strategies that make them highly effective pest catchers. You often see spider webs constructed over inverted flowerpots. As insects emerge from eggs and pupae in the soil, they fly towards the light and are immediately caught by the spider as they come through the hole in the flowerpot.

Glow worms

Although increasingly rare, you sometimes see glow worms at the edge of fields or woodland, or at garden margins. These are beautiful little creatures, and also helpful, as their larvae live on slugs and snails.

If you put a caterpillar or cocoon in a jar, you sometimes find not a butterfly but some quite different insects inside the jar later. These will be parasitoids that were living on the original species, now hatched and looking for prey.

Mini-wasps hatching out of a host cabbage caterpillar ▶

Unfortunately, many people don't particularly like spiders, but they are fierce predators, constantly on the look out for food. There are hundreds of spiders in every garden, and dozens of different species, but they are all gardeners' friends as they attack many pests including most flies, spider mites, aphids and moths.

Slow worms

Snakes are rare in British gardens, and the easily identified adder with a V-shaped mark on its head is the only poisonous snake in the British Isles. Much more common are slow worms, shiny metallic brown snake-like creatures with a marked stripe on their back and darker brown sides. Shy creatures, they live in dark, quiet places such as under large stones, or in dry stone walls. They are very good friends to any gardener as their main diet is slugs.

Wasps and predacious wasps

Even ordinary garden wasps are excellent predators. They can bring over two hundred flies per hour to a single nest to feed their young.

Other even more welcome wasps don't sting. Sometimes called mini-wasps, these tiny insects are parasitoids, using host insects as part of their own life-cycle. The ichneumonid and braconid wasps attack their hosts by laying eggs on or inside a developing insect, most choosing the larvae of insect pests including cabbage caterpillars. Their eggs develop into maggot-like larvae and eat the prey, sooner or later killing it. The only sign these mini-wasps are active in your garden may be the sight of a dead insect with tiny pinholes in it.

Parasitoids are usually restricted in the species that they can attack but once they find a population of their preferred insect hosts they provide very effective insect control as they aggressively attempt to wipe out the whole population.

PLANTING TO REPEL PESTS

Companion planting is sometimes criticised because it seems more rooted in ancient folklore than modern science, but it is usually effective, and can make gardening even more interesting.

Plant rows of beans between brassicas, and cabbage root fly and mealy aphids won't destroy a cabbage crop. This also seems to discourage blackflies from the beans. Plant sage or thyme near brassicas to put flea beetles off the scent.

Powdered wormwood (*Artemisia absinthium*) repels a number of pests, but don't sprinkle wormwood near brassicas as it inhibits their growth.

When plants grow in the right conditions, in fertile soil, pest problems will be minimised. One way of ensuring the right conditions is to use plants to influence each other by planting certain combinations.

Plant companionship works on many levels: plants can support each other by adding fertility to the soil, by offering protection from weather, from weeds and from pests and diseases. Plants keep pests away from others by producing chemicals that repel insects, by exuding a smell that puts plant-specific pests off the scent of the plants they are looking to colonise, and by attracting pests and trapping them.

Specific plants also provide a perfect breeding ground or food for helpful insects, so even when you are keeping the pest population down by planting repellent plants, you must also plant flowers to attract pest predators (see page 28) to control the pests that will break through your defences.

Homegrown warfare

Marigolds (*Tagetes spp.*) are often quoted as miracle working companion plants, keeping pests, diseases and weeds out of your garden. They do have an important role to play in pest control, as long as they are included as part of good garden practice. Marigolds produce a root exudation or secretion that discourages soil nematodes, tiny eelworms that attack and infest the roots of many plants. If you have a nematode problem in a vegetable bed, try planting a solid block of marigolds for a whole season and turning it into the soil like a green manure.

Members of the Allium family – garlic, onions, leeks, chives – seem to repel pest insects and prevent diseases. There's more research to be done, but one reason this seems to work is because Alliums donate excess minerals, including sulphur, to the soil, and excrete enzymes from their roots that seem to be toxic to many pests.

Scent deterrents

The strong scent of Alliums also repels insects that hunt by smell, as does the smell of the flowers and foliage of marigolds – particularly deterring whitefly and fleabeetle. Plant a clump of flowers for good results.

Most insects hate the strong bitter smell of rue (*Ruta graveolens*), it is particularly effective at keeping aphids away, and will even play a part in keeping four-legged pests off your garden if you plant it near entrances or around borders. Other strongly scented plants seem to confuse rather than repel insects that hunt by smell, which is why it's a good idea to plant strongly scented herbs near your brassicas or carrots to keep fleabeetles and carrot flies away.

Mint (*Mentha spp.*) repels many insect pests, including the cabbage butterfly – plant mint and the equally effective tansy (*Tanacetum officinalis*) in containers rather than in a vegetable bed as they are too invasive for open ground. Any herbs that give off strongly scented oils, such as lavender (*Lavandula spp.*), sage (*Salvia officinalis*) and rosemary (*Rosmarinus officinalis*) will deter many pest insects, while attracting some beneficial ones. Wormwood (*Artemisia absinthium*) is also excellent.

Plants to lure pests

Just as beneficial insects are attracted to specific plants, some plants are irresistible to pests. You can use this knowledge to trap insects on sacrificial plants, keeping your crops clean. Aphids, for example, can't keep away from nasturtiums, so they make good companions for apple trees and beans. The weed sowthistle (*Sonchus oleraceus*) lures leafminers as well as the lettuce root aphid. Pull it up in early summer and you'll remove numerous pests with it. You'll need to clear a patch of ground thoroughly that has been infested with sowthistle or pests and diseases will overwinter in remaining roots.

Catnip (*Nepeta cataria*) smells too strong for many insect pests.

If lemon basil (*Ocimum citriodora*) is planted in the garden close to tomatoes, it not only improves the taste of the tomatoes but deters white flies as well.

Powdered rue (*Ruta graveolens*) is an effective cat, dog and insect repellent, but it also seems to deter beneficial insects, it harms basil and slows the growth of tomatoes.

Yellow flowers attract insects to vegetable beds where they can be caught in the flowers or on sticky traps and destroyed.

The shoo-fly plant (*Nicandra physaloides*) is useful around greenhouses to attract and kill whiteflies.

Tobacco plants (*Nicotiana alata*) attract whitefly.

Broad beans attract red spider mites.

PLANTING TO ATTRACT FRIENDS

Hoverflies and bees are apparently most attracted to blue/pink/red plants while many pest insects go for yellow. Butterflies are attracted by pheromones, not colour.

Early flowering plants such as wallflowers (*Erysimum cheiri*) and pot marigolds (*Calendula officinalis*) help beneficials get established early in your garden.

Fennel ▶

Any pollen- and nectar-rich plants, such as yarrow and clover, will attract useful pollinators as well as predators. So it is important to mix and match your planting, maintaining a wide variety of plants that flower and fruit at different times. Even if your garden is largely down to productive crops, you should include some flowers, or let some crops flower. Predator wasps, for example, are particularly drawn to the flowering heads of parsley (*Petroselinum crispum*), and to flowering dill (*Anethum graveolens*) and fennel (*Foeniculum vulgare*) which also attract hoverflies and other beneficial insects.

Keep a patch of nettles (*Urtica dioica*) somewhere on the edge of your vegetable patch. Nettles are the breeding ground for the earliest hatching aphids, nettle aphids, which provide spring food for ladybirds coming out of hibernation. This means that your aphid-predator population gets going fast. To extend it at the other end of the season, ladybirds also love golden rod (*Solidago officinalis*) and morning glory (*Convolvulus tricolor*).

Hoverflies and members of the bee and wasp family are attracted to many flowers, so diversity is the key, but try and find space for buckwheat (*Fagopyrum esculentum*) and phacelia (*Phacelia tanacetifolia*). As green manures, both these plants also have useful weed-suppressing and fertility-enhancing qualities.

Herbal lures
Strongly scented herbs attract many beneficial insects as well as deterring pests (see page 27). Borage (*Borago officinalis*) attracts bees and predator wasps, and it also repels several harmful beetles. Hyssop (*Hyssopus officinalis*) attracts bees, hoverflies and lacewings and seems to repel cabbage butterflies. Lavenders (*Lavandula spp.*) and mints (*Mentha spp.*) are also favourite plants for helpful insects; Tansy (*Tanacetum vulgare*) attracts ladybirds while discouraging ants and many soil pests.

PHYSICAL CONTROLS

Planting and good gardening practices are the first lines of defence against pests. But this may not solve all your pest problems, and you may also need to get physical. There are ways of making it difficult for pests to get to their favourite plants, and ways of despatching them when they do appear. You need to be vigilant and put physical controls into place before any pest problem gets out of hand,

Identify the problem

Catching pests early is half the battle, so watch out for the first signs of pest damage and see if you can identify the problem by finding the pest or recognising the symptoms (see pages 42-58 for common problems). If you suspect a pest, check plants at different times of the day and evening as many pests come out at night.

Handpicking

Your hands are the most effective controllers for slow-moving pests. Whenever you see a pest insect just pick it up and squash it between your forefinger and thumb.

Handpicking works best on slow-moving insects, and on eggs and larvae. You can often find masses of eggs or caterpillars on the undersides of leaves, and larvae of many soil pests are often not far below the surface. Increase your chances of finding pests by creating special habitats for them – lay down some boards or piles of rotting vegetation for slugs to crawl under, earwigs will crawl into tubes or under rotting logs – then harvest them each morning.

If pests are too big to squash, drown them in a bucket of water with some vegetable soap added. You can compost them later. Handpicking is best in early morning and evening, when it is coolest and dampest, or mount torchlight patrols to pick slugs off your plants when they are most active.

Barriers

The next best method is to erect barriers to stop pests in their tracks. These need to be put in place before a pest becomes a problem – it's too late when a pest has already colonised your crop. Sticky bands or tree grease around trees will prevent climbing insects such as gypsy moth larvae from climbing treetrunks, and prevent ant damage. Wrap and tie a heavy sticky paper band around the tree about 30cm off the ground. Keep the sticky side off the bark.

Gritty barriers make life difficult for slimy bodied slugs and snails, and fences may be the only way to keep four-footed pests out. You need to dig a fence firmly into the ground, burying 30-45cm to deter burrowing creatures. If you have serious rabbit problems you can buy electric fencing, but it is expensive and grass must be kept short around it or the fence will be constantly shorting out.

Horticultural fleece and lighweight covering fabric let in air, rainwater and light but are impenetrable by small insect pests such as fleabeetles. Fleece also helps to warm the ground earlier in spring and keeps developing plants snug so that they are more resistant to any kind of stress. You can remove fleece when plants are growing strongly, but some gardeners keep covers on all season. If crops need pollination, you must remember to remove the covers for an hour or two each day.

Collars of card, foil or carpet underlay around seedlings keep many soil pests at bay. Chopped off plastic bottles protect vulnerable seedlings from most pests. Carrotflies never seem to fly higher than 60cm so a slightly taller barrier of very fine netting or polythene offers reliable protection.

Some fruit trees – particularly cherries – and soft fruit bushes will need to be netted if you want to get your fruit before the birds. If you don't net whole trees, cover bunches of grapes, or individual peaches and apricots with nets or brown paper bags as they ripen.

Traps and bait

If you wear a yellow shirt on a sultry day before thunder you'll know just how many small flying insects are attracted to yellow. Sticky squares of yellow card hung above rows of vegetables may be all you need to keep many aphids, whiteflies and fleabeetles off your vegetables. Yellow trap plants will attract them into a vegetable patch – then you can remove the plant plus its pests.

Pheromone traps (see page 39) emit chemicals that attract males of particular species to the traps with the lure of sex. They are most useful to monitor the population of orchard pests such as codling moths.

Food and drink traps are part of the pest controller's armoury. Like many creatures, slugs find alcohol highly attractive so pots of beer sunk into the ground, with the rims slightly above ground level, entice them to drink, and they drown. Where wasps become a nuisance you can trap them in jam jars filled with sugary water. Or trap pests by providing a meal of their favourite food, then picking and crushing or drowning them. Wireworms, for example, can be trapped by baits of potatoes or carrots.

You can also trap pests by providing refuges for them – earwigs will happily crawl into a cardboard tube in daytime, from where they can be gathered and disposed of.

Scaring pests away

Bird scarers, including scarecrows and mirrors in trees, have their place, and there's a theory that some animal pests will be frightened away if you mark your garden with the scent of their predators. Human hair in their path is said to deter rabbits and moles, and lion dung may keep cats and deer out. Elephant dung has been sold to repel badgers, though they seem unlikely predators! Cats will apparently flee from an inner tube masquerading as a snake! Don't rely on these, but they may help as part of a wider strategy.

Sticky traps

Make hanging traps by covering squares of card with something that stays sticky such as tree grease. If traps are to be placed on the ground next to plants, or around their stems or trunks, purchase special vegetable or horticultural grease from garden centres or mail order catalogues. Sticky tapes are also available.

Slug traps

Many creatures beside slugs like beer including hoverflies, beetles, bees and hedgehogs. Traps must include a twig so helpful creatures can crawl out of the brew, and some sort of cover to keep hedgehogs off the brew.

Sound advice

Badgers, foxes and deer apparently keep clear if they can hear human voices at night, so you could try leaving a radio on.

BOTANICAL PESTICIDES

Some plants make effective pest controllers when they're harvested, but just because an insecticide is derived from a plant, this doesn't mean it is safe for humans and other mammals – strychnine is plant-derived, but you wouldn't want to get too close to that. The botanical insecticide nicotine, for example, from (*Nicotiana tabacum*), works on insects' nervous systems so they convulse and die; humans can also be at risk if they are exposed to high doses of nicotine. Plant-derived poisons are safe in the garden because, regardless of how toxic they are, they break down into harmless compounds within hours or days when exposed to sunlight. And they are easily decomposed by soil organisms.

Pyrethrum, derris and garlic

Pyrethrum, made from the dried and powdered flowers of the pyrethrum daisy (*Chrysanthemum cinerariaefolium*), is one of the safest botanical insecticides as it harms specific pests and doesn't hurt mammals. Its active ingredient, pyrethrin, paralyses insects with an almost instant knockdown effect. Use pyrethrum against aphids, fleabeetles and small caterpillars. Look for pure powdered pyrethrum. Formulations that include piperonyl butoxide shouldn't be introduced to an organic garden.

Derris dust is made from the powdered roots of the Derris species. It kills insects on contact and acts as a stomach poison. However, although it harms a wider range of pests than pyrethrum, including aphids, thrips, red spider mite, fleabeetles and sawfly larvae, it can also harm beneficial insects and it is poisonous to fish so don't use it near ponds or streams.

An old folk remedy says that garlic can be planted to keep insects away from plants. Garlic contains allicin and other ingredients known to have insecticidal properties. Some people say garlic is effective against aphids and cabbage caterpillars as well as several pest nematodes.

HORTICULTURAL OILS AND SOAP SPRAY

Even the safest sprays can harm some creatures and plants.

• Identify the problem and see if there is an alternative to spraying.

• Only ever spray the infested parts, so don't blanket spray.

• Soap spray must hit the pests directly to be effective so it is best to spray when adults are not so active in the cool early morning.

• Never spray in windy weather, only in still weather, so spray doesn't drift.

• Never spray where bees are working. If there are hives in your area, only ever spray in the evenings when bees have finished for the day.

• Don't use washing up liquid in place of insecticidal soap. It's not designed for pest control and it can damage plants and is illegal.

Horticultural oils have been used for centuries as a way to control pests on ornamentals and fruit trees – mineral oils were recorded by Pliny in the first century. They suffocate insects at all stages of growth by blocking their breathing holes, or penetrating the shells of insect eggs and interfering with the processes of maturation.

Modern horticultural oils can also be used on vegetable crops. Since oils act physically they are safer to use than powders and sprays that affect pests' biochemistry. However, they are a relatively short-term measure. They can harm beneficial insects at certain stages of their growth cycle, and have to be reapplied regularly to get to grips with a large problem. Also, they can clog the pores and damage the leaves of any plants that are thirsty and needing to take in water when you spray. So only use oils at the coolest time of day.

Soap and water

Insecticidal soap spray is a safe way of despatching soft-bodied insect pests including aphids, leafhoppers, mites, scale insects and mealybugs. Insecticidal soap is a vegetable-based soap containing a mixture of potassium salts. The fatty acids in the soap penetrate the covering of soft-bodied insects and damage their cell membranes.

Susceptible insects become paralysed on contact so you need to spray the pest insects directly. Other insects become paralysed for a short time, then recover. Slow-moving insects are more susceptible than those that can fly away from the spray so soap sprays don't harm adult beneficial insects.

Soaps are a good emergency measure when there is a large and obvious build-up of insects on specific plants. They are virtually nontoxic to the user (unless you ingest a large quantity), they biodegrade into the soil very fast and you can spray with them right up until harvest with no ill effects or lasting residues on the plants.

BIOLOGICAL CONTROLS

Conservation of pest predators is the most easily available biological control. But it is just one option. Sometimes it is necessary to import biological controls as well as conserving those that already exist in your garden.

Sometimes a pest problem gets out of control, particularly if a garden has been neglected for a period, or rotation hasn't been practised so there's a build-up of a specific pest. Then you may also consider importing bacteria and pathogens that prey on pests – as well as encouraging their natural insect predators. Trapping insects by luring them with pheromones is another form of biological control. These methods of control are very effective against their target pests but are highly selective, so pose no threat to the beneficial creatures or other organisms that you need to conserve in your garden.

Microbial warfare

Microbial pesticides contain living micro-organisms that kill their host pests. They are purchased as powder, sprays and granules to be reconstituted in water, then applied as liquids or sprays.

The most widely used microbial pesticide is *Bacillus thuringiensis Bt*. This is a bacterial species that only works on butterfly and moth caterpillars, and is inert until an insect eats it. Then it dissolves in the gut of susceptible insects, destroying the insects' digestive system and making holes in the gut wall. *Bt* is a useful control against the cabbage butterfly caterpillar, and some other caterpillar pests. The narrow range and specific activity of *Bt* means that no beneficial insects are killed by it and you can use it with other natural controls.

Another option is to introduce nematodes into your soil. These are tiny roundworms that prey on soil and aquatic insects and grubs, entering the bodies of their hosts and killing them by infecting them with bacteria that poison their blood. Nematodes can be effective in controlling slugs.

The main disadvantages of applying microbial controls are that they are very environment- as well as pest-specific and need a controlled environment if they are going to be successful. If the temperature or conditions of the soil fluctuate much, the bacteria will be killed off – nematodes, for example, are particularly effective in a tunnel where conditions remain relatively constant. As microbial controls only act on pests at one specific stage of their develop- ment, you need to be vigilant to apply them at the best time – once susceptible caterpillars hatch into adults *Bt* has no effect.

As microbials are living organisms, they have quite a short shelf-life compared to botanicals or other controls. They are best used as part of a wider strategy, and only use *Bt* when you have a real problem as over-use may lead to pests ultimately adapting and becoming resistant to the bacteria.

Pheromones

Pheromone controls were developed for large-scale agriculture, but they can be very useful for any size of orchard. Pheromones are chemicals secreted and released by a particular species that elicit responses in other mem- bers of the same species. Sex pheromones are released by females to attract males, and you can purchase pheromone traps to control a variety of pests including gypsy moths and codling moths. Unsuspecting adult males are lured into a sticky cardboard trap baited with pheromones, or into a container with no exit. Then they are caught and disposed of.

Sex pheromone traps alone won't necessarily control a pest population as they only attract males, so they are most useful to monitor a pest population in order to select the best way of dealing with it. They highlight pest populations rather than destroying them. A possible dis- advantage is that they may attract more pests into your garden, so never hang the traps near the pests' preferred habitats but attach them to trees around the perimeter of the garden that the pests are not normally attracted to.

Genetic engineering of microbial pesticides
Microbial insecticides are targets for research in the biotechnology industry, where researchers are increasingly focusing on genetically enhancing the toxicity of microbes rather than looking at the possibilities offered by naturally occurring micro-organisms. The aim of much of the research is to increase the speed at which microbials kill pests, to make them less environment-specific, and to develop plants resistant to pests – such as Monsanto's genetically engineered pest resistant tobacco and tomato plants. This may ultimately lead to the development of insect resistance to microbes, and a situation where *Bt* is no longer a useful insecticide.

HOW

DO I RECOGNISE AND CONTROL COMMON PESTS?

Some pests appear in nearly every garden. Learn about their life-cycles – how they breed, how fast they mature, and where they live in certain stages of development – so that you can decide on the best methods of control. Then pest control becomes common sense.

RECOGNISING THE PROBLEMS

Fruit pests

Midges, mites, sawflies and other bugs can usually be controlled through good practice: lightly cultivate the ground round trees and bushes in autumn to expose larvae and cocoons; remove mulches in autumn so there are fewer places for pests to overwinter; and remove and compost any damaged fruit immediately. If you do see pests, handpick them or spray with soap and water.

There are hundreds of species of insects in every garden, Most of them will never cause you much of a problem, so the following pages refer only to the commonest pests that you are most likely to come across, beginning with slugs and snails because these cause more obvious damage in more gardens than any other pest.

Earwigs and ants are sometimes thought of as pests but they cause little damage and can be helpful as well as destructive. If they do cause you problems trap earwigs (page 33) and dispose of them, and disturb an ant's nest by digging through it and dispersing the colony. You can prevent them from climbing plants with sticky bands and barriers (page 31).

Fruit pests

Soft fruit and tree fruit suffer from a variety of pests not found elsewhere in the garden. Codling moths are a major pest of apple and pear orchards; the caterpillars tunnel to the core of the fruits but there's no evidence until the fruit is harvested. To protect trees, keep sticky grease bands in place to prevent the larvae climbing the trunks, and hang pheromone traps (see page 39) to catch male moths. Encourage bluetits by hanging fat in trees in winter, as they are major predators and can eat 95 per cent of codling moth cocoons over the winter.

Biological control in the greenhouse

Red spider mites and whiteflies are two troublesome greenhouse pests. Spider mites are minute creatures found on the undersides of leaves. A severe infestation can kill a plant. Prevent the pests with good hygiene and maintenance, but if necessary you should purchase and introduce predatory mites (*Phytoselius persimilis*). Whitefly in the greenhouse can be controlled in the same way as other aphids (see page 54) or introduce the predatory wasps (*Encarsia formosa*).

SLUGS AND SNAILS

Slugs and snails are land-dwelling molluscs that move on one muscular foot on mucus slime trails. Most British gardeners wage a constant war against these greedy pests as they eat virtually any plant matter and can remain active almost all year where summers are damp and cool and winters warmish and wet. There is no instant way to solve a slug problem, but try a combination of methods and you should beat the pests.

Slug control
Cultivation: Slug eggs are just about everywhere in the soil, but they don't hatch unless the conditions are just right. Cultivate soil well in spring to bring them up to the surface, where they can dry out and die.

Give young plants the best chance by transplanting seedlings from modules rather than sowing straight into the ground. When you mulch, keep it pulled back away from the base of your plants. If you lay black polythene for weed control, watch out! It acts like a luxurious slug hotel, warming up the soil and keeping it moist. So don't grow young plants or vegetables anywhere near that area.

Put decaying plant matter straight onto the compost, don't leave it lying around. Keep your compost pile well away from your garden. Slugs enjoy the warm, moist compost, and help break it down.

Handpicking: Slugs hunt most hungrily in the moist evenings so mount torchlight patrols to hand pick all the slugs you find. When they're not feeding they like a warm, dark atmosphere, so pay attention to the shady areas of your garden, and look under stones and piles of rotting vegetation where they like to congregate. Turn stones over regularly and scrape off slugs and snails and their eggs. Drown them in water and feed them to ducks, or compost them. You need to handpick regularly to make a serious impact, but it is a useful control when seedlings are most vulnerable.

Slug pellets
- Don't be tempted to use slug pellets for a quick fix. They may not solve the problem and they may harm creatures other than their target pests.
- The main ingredient in most slug pellets for gardens is metaldehyde which dehydrates the slugs. However, if it rains while the slug is dehydrating – which can take a day – the pest rehydrates.
- Metaldehyde works best in hot drier conditions, which is when slug activity is lowest.
- Slug pellets get washed away in rain, they degrade in sunlight, and they only ever catch a small proportion of slugs.
- Some pellets are based on methiocarb which acts as a stomach poison.
- Only about 4% of a slug pellet is metaldehyde or methiocarb, the rest is a bait of ground cereal similar to dog food, which can attract other creatures as well as slugs.
- If something else snacks on pellets or a freshly poisoned slug, it may also be poisoned.

Predators: Encourage birds – thrushes and blackbirds particularly love snails. Encourage frogs, hedgehogs, toads and slow worms. Ground beetles eat the pests and eggs. If you have space in your garden, keep a few ducks and chickens.

Traps: Slugs love beer, and sinking shallow cartons or bowls full of beer at strategic points in your garden should encourage slugs to head for the traps rather than the plants. Only use beer traps until early summer or you risk drowning bees, too. Keep a stick in a beer trap so that ground beetles can get out.

Try leaving eaten grapefuit halves, peel side up, among your plants, and slugs will gather underneath ready for disposal, or leave small piles of chopped-up juicy lettuce or comfrey leaves to provide pre-planned meals. Place these as far away as possible from the crops you are try-ing to protect, or you'll find the pests just move on to your other plants for pudding.

Barriers: Spread gritty protective barriers on the soil sur-face. These will need to be reapplied virtually each time it rains. Slugs and snails won't cross copper or they get small electric shocks, and don't like aluminium foil, so copper wire, copper backed tape or foil collars round your favourite plants could do the trick.

Biological control: You can buy nematodes that destroy slugs – put these microscopic parasites into the soil. *Phasmarhabdites hermaphrodita* enter the body of a slug and multiply inside them so that their host swells to a size where it no longer feeds, then burrows deep into the ground and dies.

Covers: To protect individual young plants and seedlings, make some fine wire mesh covers and place them over the plants. Glass or plastic cloches are also helpful and you can also use the tops of cut-off plastic bottles but you have to be careful to move them when it's hot or you may roast your plants.

Barriers

- *Ash*: Wood ash not only keeps slugs off but is an excellent feed for tomatoes. But avoid solid fuel ash and soot as they can contain small amounts of toxins that can alter the soil balance.
- *Bran*: A tempting snack which forms an absorbent and deathly barrier.
- *Grit* (not for sandy soils): Fine grit also makes an attractive anti-pest mulch for plants in containers.
- *Sawdust* (not for clay soils where it can cause nitrogen starvation): Use sawdust from wood untreated with chemical preservatives.
- *Copper or foil barriers*: copper tapes are now available that give slugs a small electric shock when they cross them.
- *Eggshells*: Baking these shells before crushing makes them stronger, sharper and longer-lasting.
- *Seafood shells*: You can buy these shells from garden centres or pound your own. They are very decorative as well as repellent around ornamental plants.

COMMON PESTS – APHIDS

Some aphids are plant-specific; others move from one plant to another, and they can easily spread viruses if their mouthparts get contaminated. Some plants don't get much affected by the aphids; others produce twisted, curled or swollen leaves or stems. Occasionally, aphids may actually kill leaves. They excrete masses of honeydew when they feed, which turns into black sooty mould on leaves and stems, and attracts ants, flies and wasps which can then become a nuisance. Although plants look rough when covered with sooty moulds, these don't damage the plant tissues. Once the aphids disappear, the sooty mould often dries up and falls off the plant.

Aphids are tremendous reproducers. The females give birth to tiny female nymphs that start sucking sap immediately, and the cycle of their birth to adulthood and producing new aphids only takes 10-14 days. So they tend to constantly reinfest plants. Some aphids have very complex life histories, living on several different host plants and overwintering on different species.

Aphids are sap-sucking insects found on many varieties of plant. They are widespread but not hard to control.

Common aphids

Blackfly start on the tips of plants – favouring broad beans, nasturtiums, thistles and their relatives – then spread downwards. A severe infestation can spoil a crop of beans.

Greenfly are most troublesome on ornamentals, especially roses where they can damage the buds.

Mealy aphids look as though they have been dusted with grey flour. They infest brassicas and cause distorted and discoloured leaves.

Woolly aphids protect themselves by producing a downy coating. They commonly infest apple trees, attracting ants and wasps and often harbouring disease.

Lettuce root aphids prevent lettuce plants from developing fully.

Aphid controls

Cultivation: make sure plants are given best conditions and don't use too much nitrogen as this produces sappy growth which encourages aphids.

Predators: Encourage predators by planting attractant plants (page 28) – ladybirds, hoverflies, lacewings, predacious wasps and earwigs prey on aphids.

Barriers: Using fleece or other row covers can protecet against aphids and the diseases they transmit.

Handpicking: Squash on sight.

Companion planting: Plant nasturtiums with apple trees for aphid hosts. Plant wallflowers in orchards for early supplies of nectar so that predators such as lacewings and hoverflies can get going early.

Resistance: Grow resistant varieties of lettuces.

Spraying: soap and water. Hose woolly aphis with jets of cold water.

CATERPILLARS, CUTWORMS, EELWORMS

Caterpillars

The large white or cabbage caterpillar is familiar to everyone who grows brassicas – or verbascums. The cabbage white butterfly lays eggs on the undersides of leaves in May and July. The resulting yellow and black caterpillars feed hungrily, often completely stripping a plant of its leaves.

Cutworms

The larvae of a group of moths, fat brown cutworms are up to 30mm long. Suspect them if your seedlings are nipped off at or near the ground. Cutworm larvae start foraging in early spring. They eat at night, feeding on underground stems and roots and spend the day under surface litter near plant stems or in burrows in the top few inches of soil. Some species overwinter as eggs, others as larvae or adult moths. There can be up to four generations a year.

Eelworms

Eelworms are species of tiny transparent nematodes that attack tomatoes, potatoes and cucumbers as well as some ornamentals.

Cabbage caterpillar control

Cultivation: Don't leave brassica stumps in the ground over winter. Grow brassicas with plenty of compost – this seems to help plants to recover from any infestation.

Predators: Encourage predacious wasps – the ichneumon wasp lays its eggs in the bodies of the caterpillars.

Hand picking: caterpillars are easy to find and pick off. Throw them into a bucket of water to drown them, then compost them.

Companion planting: Aromatic herbs seem to deter the butterflies so plant sage and wormwood near the brassicas, or place some pots of lavender and mint among your cabbages. Hyssop may attract the butterflies away from crop plants.

Biological controls: Use *Bt* as your last resort.

Cutworm control

Cultivation: Cutworms eat the roots of grasses and weeds as well as seedlings, so keep your ground clear of weeds, start seedlings in modules and transplant them later.

Barriers: Surround young plants with collars of cardboard, newspaper or even carpet underlay to protect them until they are strong enough to withstand attack.

Handpicking: Clear the ground around seedlings in early morning and you can often find cutworms curled up into a C shape. Rake them up and drown them. Gently scratch away the top 5cm of soil to find more in shallow burrows.

Predators: Ground beetles and birds feed on cutworms. They are hosts for some predacious wasps.

Eelworm control

Cultivation is the key to reducing eelworm. They are destroyed by mycelium-forming fungi, so soil that is well-enriched with compost is a bad habitat for eelworms.

Companion planting: Root exudations of African marigolds (*Tagetes erecta*) kill pest nematodes.

CARROT FLY & ONION FLY

Carrot fly

(carrot root fly / carrot rust fly)
The adult fly is smaller than 5mm
with a dark body, yellow legs and
head and red eyes. Flies lay eggs in
late April and May on the soil
surface around carrot plants. The
eggs hatch in a week and the
yellowish white maggots feed on
and in carrot roots. After four to six
weeks they change into brown
pupae which hatch in late July or
August when more adult flies
emerge and lay eggs. This group
causes plant damage into autumn.
In a warm September more flies
may develop to cause late damage.
Carrot flies spend the winter as
pupae in the soil or as maggots in
the roots.

Onion flies

Resembling small houseflies, they
emerge from the soil in May to lay
their eggs on the soil surface near
suitable plants. The emerging white
maggots can be up to 1cm long, and
they feed for three weeks on onion
roots before pupating. Young plants
can die, leaves of older plants wilt
and the flies damage onion bulbs
which are then likely to rot. Like the
carrot fly, there may be two or three
generations a year.

Carrot fly control

The maggots of this small fly can destroy your carrot crop, and may also attack parsnips, celery and celeriac. Affected plants may become stunted but usually the plant tops continue to look healthy. You know you've got problems if your carrots have dark patches and small rusty coloured tunnels through them.

Cultivation: You'll have least problems in light soil that is not overmanured. In some areas you can sow early to avoid the main egg-laying period; otherwise sow late after the first flush of adults have emerged and dispersed. Wherever possible sow resistant varieties. Never leave carrots in the ground in autumn but lift them all in October so the pests can't overwinter.

Companions: Plant chives beside carrots to deter the flies.

Barriers: Cover rows of carrots with either horticultural fleece or fine mesh covers. Carrot flies don't fly higher than 60cm so erect barriers of polythene or fine mesh around the crops.

Onion fly control

Onion fly pupae can remain dormant in the soil for many years, and can devastate an onion crop.

Cultivation: Try to sow onions before May when there is the least chance of damage. Plant onion sets rather than sowing seeds as plants are most susceptible as young seedlings. Dig infected land in winter to disturb the overwintering populations of the fly. Make sure you practise rotation.

Barriers: Grow under a protective cover of fleece or row covering fabric.

Companion planting: Onion flies hunt by scent so growing parsley and strong-scented herbs with or around onion crops can help.

CRANEFLIES, FLEABEETLES, LEAFMINERS

Fleabeetles

These small black flying beetles can be a real nuisance in hot dry summers. They arrive in clouds and can eat a row of young brassica seedlings overnight and make serious holes in the leaves of larger plants. The first batch appears in May to June, when temperatures reach around 20°C, the second batch in August.

Leafminers

These greenish-white grubs about 20mm long infest many leafy vegetables, particularly spinach and beet. Flies lay eggs on leaf undersides. These hatch within 4 days and the larvae eat threadlike winding tunnels within the leaves. As feeding continues the tunnels join together to make large light coloured blotches filled with darker waste matter. Four generations are possible in a single season.

Craneflies

The larvae of craneflies/daddylonglegs can become a nuisance as they eat the roots of grass in lawns and can easily defoliate large patches.

Handpicking: Soak the lawn and cover it overnight with damp newspaper or carpet. In the morning lift the cover and grubs will have been brought to the surface. Drown and compost them.

Predators: Many birds feast on them, but they can also attract moles and even badgers into your garden.

Fleabeetle control

Fleabeetles hunt in droves and can decimate a crop of young brassicas overnight by drilling the leaves full of tiny holes.

Cultivation and barriers: Careful timing of your sowing and planting can prevent the worst problems. Plant early if possible, under cloches or fleece, and cover germinating seedlings with fleece or lightweight row-covering fabric. Plant fast-growing brassicas again in July when the fleabeetles are dormant. Keep young plants well watered.

Traps: Hang yellow sticky traps above rows of brassicas to attract the beetles. If you run your hand over plants twice daily you'll catch large numbers as fleabeetles jump up when disturbed.

Botanicals: Use derris dust as a last resort.

Leafminer control

Leafminers are the larvae of various small flies, beetles and moths. They don't do too much harm, although they can check growth on young plants and make mature leaves very unsightly.

Cultivation: Dig in winter to destroy overwintering pests.

Barriers: Covers of horticultural fleece or row-covering material can prevent the insects getting a hold. Always pick off affected leaves.

VINE WEEVILS

Vine weevils

Vine weevil larvae are serious pests of a wide variety of plants. They are most often found in the compost of bought-in container-grown plants, but can also attack plants in open ground, particularly fuchsia, primulas, cyclamen and begonias. Most houseplants are also at risk. Vine weevils devour the roots of their victims, but the first sign is not a creeping pest but usually a wilting plant that cannot be revived. Plants often keel right over or a gentle tug is all it takes to remove them from their compost or soil to reveal an absence of roots, and plump white grubs curled up in the container or 5cm below the soil surface.

Watch out: Whenever you introduce a new container plant take it from its pot and check thoroughly for weevils and their larvae. If a plant, outdoors or indoors, wilts suddenly, check the root system without delay. If caught in time, plants can be saved through repotting or replanting. Never re-use infected compost unless you sterilise it well. Clean all pots thoroughly at the end of the season.

Cultivation: Dig ground in winter to bring grubs near to the surface where conditions are too cold for them to survive, and birds can take them.

Handpicking: Adult vine weevils are relatively slow-moving and if you disturb them they usually lie on their backs and pretend to be dead so you can easily handpick them. All larvae should be dropped into hot water and destroyed.

Barriers: Put a strip of wide tape around individual pots and tubs, and smear this liberally with a non-drying glue which the weevils cannot cross.

Biological control: You can buy nematodes that control vine weevils, but success depends on fairly constant temperature and soil conditions, and a plentiful supply of weevil larvae.

Adult vine weevils are matt black, about 1cm long, with a noticeable snout. They don't fly but climb to make holes and irregular notches in plant foliage. It is their larvae that are the real pests. These are up to 1cm long with a plump, creamy white body and a brown head. Female vine weevils emerge in early spring. Over a 3-4 month period they lay hundreds of eggs on the soil surface close to host plants. The larvae emerge after about 2 weeks, then tunnel into the soil, feeding on plant roots. As the weather cools in autumn larvae burrow to overwinter at a greater depth, and when it warms up in spring they pupate, and new adults crawl from the soil 3-4 weeks later.

In homes and heated glasshouses consistent warmth will enable weevils to be active all year round and to complete their life-cycle more quickly.

WHITEFLIES & WIREWORMS

Whiteflies
Often categorised with aphids, whiteflies have sucking mouthparts and feed on plant sap. They usually rest and feed on the undersides of leaves and fly off when disturbed. Affected plants have wilted leaves and are often coated with sooty moulds but whiteflies rarely cause lasting damage.

Wireworms
These are a particular menace when you are gardening on recently converted old pasture land. Click beetles lay their eggs in summer and the larvae will feed in March to May and in September and October for up to five years before turning into beetles and flying elsewhere. They don't like to be disturbed so they feed quite deep in the soil, and one of the strategies for control is to provide lures to bring them nearer the surface.

Wireworm ▶

Controlling whiteflies

Many species of whitefly – small flying insects about 2mm long – are common pests in the greenhouse, on houseplants, and on brassicas. The small white-winged insects live on the undersides of leaves, and plants can look as though they've been dusted with ash.

Cultivation: Good soil management and rotation will keep whiteflies at bay, and break the cycle of cabbage aphids by removing all plants in autumn.

Predators: Encourage the many aphid-predators with attractant plants.

Handpicking: Vacuum whiteflies off houseplants.

Spraying: Spray with soapy water or just use a hose – the water must hit the insects directly to have any effect.

Controlling wireworms

Wireworms are the slim orange-brown larvae of the click beetle, which can be up to 2.5cm long. They feed on roots and underground parts of grasses and vegetables. When you clear grass away they will feed on whatever comes next, particularly potatoes and other root crops.

Cultivation: When you clear old pasture land it is a good idea to grow a green manure crop of mustard (*Brassica nigra*) before planting vegetables. This encourages the wireworms to feed nearer the surface, and when you turn it under the soil in spring the larvae feed on it so greedily that they complete their life-cycle in record time and fly away to lay eggs in grassland elsewhere. Harvest crops by September to limit damage from autumn feeding.

Predators: Cultivation encourages wireworms near the surface where birds can feed on them.

Traps: In small areas trap wireworms by punching holes in old food cans and filling them with bait of potato and carrot peelings or pieces of potato. Bury the cans so their tops are at ground level. Empty the trapped wireworms and drown them every two weeks or so.

BIRDS, CATS & MOLES

Birds get wise to bird scarers, so you must change them regularly. It is reported that scarecrows are most effective if they are dressed in red!

In the eighteenth century, a popular gardening manual suggested the best way to make moles leave a garden: 'Take red herrings and cutting them in pieces burn the pieces on the molehills or put garlicke or leeks in the mouths of their Hill and the mole will leave the ground.'

Birds

Your garden needs birds to eat many insect pests and aerate the soil, so welcome them, but keep them off your seedlings with barriers, or scare them off soft fruit bushes and vulnerable crops. Cover rows of young seedlings with chicken wire or cloches, and net fruit, or rig up webs of black thread. Birds will get used to most scaring devices so you need to change them regularly but half potatoes with feathers stuck into them seem to keep them off seedlings. Rows of jangling metal rods, old CDs or flapping strips of plastic keep some birds away. Or you can buy commercial humming line to stretch above rows of vegetables – it glints and makes a noise in the wind.

Cats

Cats are a nuisance because they use your garden as a toilet. Find their toilet spots, clear away all the top layer of soil to remove the scent, and stick short sharp twigs all over the area. You may have to do this several times to persuade the cats to go elsewhere. Reportedly you can keep them off your borders by draping a piece of hosepipe or inner tube in their favourite plants – apparently they think the tubes are snakes, and disappear fast.

Moles

Moles eat quantities of millipedes, cranefly larvae and wireworms, but they also eat earthworms and they can do a lot of damage uprooting plants by burrowing under them. They hunt by smell so you can send moles away by finding the end of a mole run, digging down until you see the tunnel and laying garlic, onions or even old fish there before covering it up. Or try sticking partly buried empty bottles in the most recent molehills, or childrens' seaside windmills, and the sounds and vibrations may deter the moles. If this doesn't work, you may need to catch them in specially designed mole traps.

MICE & RABBITS, BADGERS & DEER

All animals hunt by scent, so you can often keep them at bay by introducing or mimicking the scent of their predators.

Badgers can be lured to another part of the garden with supplies of rotting fruit.

It is illegal to shoot or trap badgers or wild deer – it is also illegal to pick up any animals that you run over on the road, but it's all right for the driver behind to take them.

Mice
Field mice can steal the seeds of early spring and autumn sowings of peas and beans, and eat many bulbs as well as nibbling root vegetables. Use physical barriers of thorny twigs, but the best course is to catch the mice in humane traps or get a cat.

Rabbits
If young plants are chewed to the roots, and your vegetables disappear overnight, you've got rabbits. The only way to keep them out is with secure fencing, or you may have nothing left in your vegetable patch, and no young plants in your borders. Construct a sturdy wire mesh fence using maximum 5cm mesh. Dig a trench 30cm deep on the outside of the fence and firmly bury that depth of wire. If you can't fence, try tying clumps of human hair to sticks around your vegetables – rabbits don't like the smell.

Badgers and deer
Once a badger has located your vegetable plot he will use it as his local deli and keep returning nightly, shifting almost anything you put in his way. Badgers also make a mess of your lawn, digging for cranefly larvae and leaving masses of calling cards. Tying oil or creosote-soaked rags around the perimeter of your garden can deter them, and they don't like disturbance so humming wires and jangling chimes can put them off. But if possible you should fence securely, nailing boards to the bottom of the fence and about 60cm up.

Deer eat young trees and shrubs. Fencing them out of a garden is a mammoth task. Instead you need to protect all young trees with deer guards and preferably wooden and mesh cages – this also protects young plants from rabbits. Dumping lion dung around your garden perimeter is supposed to help, but the jury's out on this one.

RESOURCES

Organisations to join

Centre for Alternative Technology (CAT)
Machynlleth
Powys SY20 9AZ
01654 702400
info@cat.org.uk

HDRA, the organic organisation
Ryton Gardens
Ryton on Dunsmore
Coventry
Warwickshire CV8 3LG
024 7630 3517
enquiry@hdra.org.uk

Soil Association
Bristol House
40-56 Victoria Street
Bristol BS1 6BY
0117 929 0661
info@soilassociation.org

Gardening on the web

Centre for Alternative Technology (CAT)
www.cat.org.uk

HDRA, the organic organisation
www.hdra.org.uk

Organic UK
www.organic.mcmail.com

Soil Association
www.soilassociation.org

Mail order

Chase Organics
Riverdene Business Park
Molesey Road
Horsham
Surrey KT12 4RG
01932 253666
www.OrganicCatalog.com
suppliers of seeds, tools and equipment

More books to read

Bob Flowerdew, *The Companion Garden*, Kyle Cathie, 1991

Peter Harper, *Natural Garden Book*, Gaia Books, 1994

William and Helga Olkowski, *Common Sense Pest Control*, Taunton Press, 1995

Pauline Pears and Sue Stickland, *RHS Organic Gardening*, Octopus, 1995

John Seymour, *The Complete Book of Self Sufficiency*, Dorling Kindersley, 1997

Bob Sherman and Pauline Pears, *Pests: How to control them on fruit and vegetables*, HDRA/Search Press, 1992

INDEX

A GAIA ORIGINAL

Books from Gaia celebrate the vision of Gaia, the self-sustaining living Earth, and seek to help its readers live in greater personal and planetary harmony.

Design   Lucy Guenot, Mark Epton
Editor   Pip Morgan
Index   Mary Warren
Photography   Steve Teague except pages 2 and 23
Production   Lyn Kirby
Direction   Joss Pearson, Patrick Nugent

Photograhy;
page 2 © William Osborne,
page 23 © Chris Packham,
both of BBC Natural History Unit

First published in the United Kingdom in 2001 by
Gaia Books Ltd, 66 Charlotte Street, London W1T 4QE

ISBN 1 85675 127 9

A catalogue record of this book is available from the British Library.

Printed and bound in Italy

10 9 8 7 6 5 4 3 2

The Edible Container Garden

Michael Guerra ISBN 1 85675 089 2 £11.99
*Plan well, plant properly and care for your soil for maximum
produce from minimum space.*

A Heritage of Flowers

Tovah Martin ISBN 1 85675 093 0 £14.99
*This book tells of the history of old-fashioned flowers, both garden
and wild, and the importance of their continued survival.*

Heritage Vegetables

Sue Stickland ISBN 1 85675 033 7 £14.99
*A guide to collecting, exchanging and cultivating old-fashioned
vegetable seeds, and why you should choose to grow them.*

The Gaia Natural Garden

Peter Harper ISBN 1856751732   £14.99
*A beautiful guide to harmonizing gardening with the natural world.
Foreword by Geoff Hamilton.*

The Rothschild Gardens

Miriam Rothschild et al ISBN 1 85675 112 0 £16.99
*Wildflower meadows, parks and gardens created by the Rothschilds.
Photography by Andrew Lawson.*

To order a book please phone: 01476 541 080 or fax: 01476 541 061
If you would like further details on Gaia titles please contact:
Gaia Books Ltd, 66 Charlotte Street, London, W1T 4QE
Tel: 020 7323 4010   Fax: 020 7323 0435
website: www.gaiabooks.co.uk